Jeanne Farr

Thank you for loving my poetry
as much as I do.

The Meaning of Me

A Book of Poetry

emmett wheatfall

Reflections Publishing House
Inglewood, CA

ewheatfall@gmail.com
P.O. Box 30105
Portland, OR 97294

Cover Design by – Luo American, Inc.

ISBN 978-0-9837231-4-1
Library of Congress Control Number 2012942136
First Printing, June 2012

Printed in the United States of America

Reflections Publishing House
PO Box 294, Inglewood, CA
www.reflectionspublishings.net

I sat with fools
who hung on every word—
and they crowned me their king.

-emmett wheatfall

Contents

The Meaning of Me

As I take to toil in hand
The finer points of pen
Deeper I delve
Into the meaning of me

Wherein

I shall call to it
And it shall come
The meaning of me
It shall come

Swan

A swan just leaped from the marsh
With its wings spread wide
Like love
Beneath fluffy clouds—
White as lilies
Into blue
The spacious sky

Watchful Eyes

Nearby

a swan bathes
quietly

under watchful eyes

nearby

Whirlwinds

where whirlwinds
once whined in constant
crumpled leaves
no longer leap in pageant
scurrying landscape
like carpenter ants
tumbling acrobatically
with such *advent*

In The Spring

There is neither
hope nor despair;
yet, she still laughs,
under
the Juniper Tree,
in the spring,
while the birds
all rally in song.

Bristling Bee

A bee bristles

Before the Blue Petunia

The sun doesn't mind

They rule the day

Old Black Raven

Old Black Raven

Un-nest the quieted prey
Bring death oh merchant thereof
To the sick, weak, the young

Mercy, mercy, where are you?
Pity, where have you parted?
Only the living can conjecture

Old Black Raven

Strike suddenly silent stalker
Rend from mother her seedling
Make mockery of easy the meal

Grace, grace, where are you?
Empathy, where have you parted?
Only the living can conjecture

Old Black Raven

Spring

Spring comes caustically, wearing a sundress,
incessantly intruding upon the fading froth of
winter's lips and chilled body.

As winter warms spring's oppression becomes bigger.
All the while mother nature nurtures her dignity in
unambiguous silence.

A dandelion has the nerve to lift her head, wearing
the gold fedora, breaking the surface of the cold and
weakened earth.

Spring always sends her, this emissary, empowered
to negotiate terms, backed up by the immense power
of the terse sun, whose anxious nature is, heightened
anxiety.

Others will come wearing the gold fedora, edging out
the frothy grass. And the terse sun will settle in the
sky— everyday.

Lighthouse

rolling waves…
weave the sea,
over and under
the lighthouse
reef.
O' breath of
silent shores,
timid tumult
the lighthouse
ignores.

Pen For Me

emmett,

pen for me a love poem
in iambic pentameter; a lovely sonnet
in the clouds of day and the stars
of night.

Pen for me a lyrical melody
in prose so sweet; the heavens revel
and earth trembles for poetry's
sake.

emmett,

pen for me something silly;
something syllabic, with a meter so sweet
it beats rhythmic and slow; like matters
truly of the heart.

Pen for me verse as wild as your eyes
caressing the sensual silhouette of a ceramic
bust, on display, in full view
of you its poetic lover.

Pen for me.
Pen for me emmett—

pen for me.

Eden

There is distance between us,
you and I: spatial, measured,

and guarded.

Unwritten is the covenant
governing our coveting; still,

we meet,

in the midst of the garden,
Eden, our garden our world,

ours alone; we,
the two of us, alone.

Blind is the unsuspecting
world, the secret in ours,

a hidden world.

When passing we glance,
sometimes we dance,

contrived

with our eyes, our thoughts,
our smile.

Merry is our go-round. Fixed
is our axis, our center,

our core.

Transfixed we circle
the anxiety of admiration,

separation; controlled is our
prolonged longing.

When then is it sin? When
love is pure? Purifying the

impurities is the fire of love.

You get me, and I you.
Mystical our telepathy,

nonverbal

our communication. Words,
thought, and affections, all

together understood. The
relationship—private;

the bond—unspoken.

The Reason For Love

Is this the issue: everything is in bloom. There are
pretty palettes
and transparent materials transforming the season;
for reasons,
giving rise to unambiguous meaning.

When it comes to the blossom, live in the moment, for
there is life
living in the bloom.

Fall in love.

Fall, in love.

Fall, in, love.

Make falling, falling in love, the most memorable
moment of your life.
The more you fall the better chance you'll have for
love; for reasons,
giving rise to unambiguous meaning.

Develop the timeless touch. Avoid the sudden rush,
the flush
of sensation, when love is but a bud. Wait for the
blossom: there is life
living in the bloom. Where pretty palettes and
transparent materials
transform the season—and the reason for love.

Slightly Left Of Center

These rolling hills have come full circle, where
flowing in on western winds is a cloud; seated
slightly left of center.

That cottage in the valley brings to my remembrance
a century's old architecture and, the woman I once
loved, and choose to love again.

Red as red can possibly be is the barn
adjacent to the agitated creek running east and west.
We made lofty love there, she to me and I her.

As is the creek, I'm agitated. For, the closer I get
the further away I feel. I want to go back. I want to go
there.

There is there, beyond these rolling hills, where
I'm flowing in on western winds, and is the cottage,
and the red red barn,
where the creek is agitated, and is

the woman I choose to love, again.

Where Have All The Pretty Flowers Gone?

Tell me, where have all the pretty flowers gone?

Those flowers whose surface is as soft as the most
silent of unspoken sentiment expressed in a smile;

whose every petal is as delicate as the icing
meticulously fashioned on a dessert showcased in
a French delicatessen;

or the ones whose neck resembles the likeness of
those in a bouquet of long stem roses, freshly cut for
the fancy of someone's lover.

Where, have all the pretty flowers gone?

These pretty flowers rise when I'm sleeping;
grow together in a splendor I find quite grandiose;

whose aromatic aroma attracts like that of
Asterocampa celtis; that's butterflies for the
less informed.

Their radiance radiates like the feverish impulse of an
embellished lust, amplified by the magnitude of
two peoples' heated libido.

Where are the pretty flowers whose appearance
pushes the penmanship of authors and lyricists, who

use them as metaphors for stories of love and
triumphant;
for songs songbirds sing in Carnegie Hall and
Julliard, in churches, mosques and synagogues all
over

the world; at weddings and funerals in celebration
and in memoriam to the loved as well as the lost.

Where, have all the pretty flowers gone?

Why does the sun rise to scorch the earth where
the pretty flowers grow? Why do the pretty flowers
fade in its presence?

What mockery is to be made of this? As if
troubadours, the pretty flowers come, tell their tale,
and then they go,

leaving me to ask poetically—

Where have all the pretty flowers gone?

Venice Is Lovely That Way

she says

Venice is lovely that way
her sentiment expressed without dissension
for by tender patience I listen
as our gondola graciously streams
the viaducts of Venetian streamlets
the Grand Channel of Venetian antiquity

lovely like a tulip's touch
to the lips of a maiden
a virgin
caressed by the warmth of flesh
the sweet smell of spice
placed lightly below the pinna
under a fine mane

she says

Venice is lovely that way
her sentiment continues without dissension
under big the beautiful brolly
unfurled beneath the lagging sun
as our gondola floats
at the helm of a gondolier

affectionately placed are her words
with respect to the architecture
with their splendid design
the forethought of such Gothic brilliance
made vivid by color and form

like the shape of a strong man's chest
and the power of his impassioned eyes

she says

Venice is lovely that way
her sentiment fading with a sigh
as if overwhelmed by love
in the arms of her lovers embrace
hypnotized by the minstrel's mandolin
playing alongside the channel

for there is no fairer place than Venice
thank the gods of the Venetians
as the wisdom etched in beauty transcends
the most majestic of mountains
the modesty of the fairest woman
the strength of the fiercest warrior
who dominated Venetian fields of battle

Venice is lovely that way

she says

I Loved You Once

I loved you once

In the margins of my mind
While others occupied the text
There being no room for you there
Between the lines
Whereupon sat the black letters
Arranged as consonants and vowels
Proper names and improper nouns
Verbs as well as adjectives
Whose syntax said, no!
You cannot love her
Not now, nor forevermore

Oh! I loved you once

Outside the calligraphy
Beyond the fountain of fonts
In the margins of empty space there
Where I placed you
I contextualized you
Alone and unscripted
Augmented without words
Unimpeded by the black letters
I had you to myself
In the open recess of my mind
And the margins of my love

Yes! I loved you once

As sure as the sun rises and shines

Even as the sea ripples roll
As the black letters stand tall there
Foreshadowing things to come
Like magi who traveled from the east
These things the black letters speak
In between the lines they speak
There being no room for you there
That's why I summoned you
To the margins
To the margins of my mind

More so now

I loved you once

La Flamingo

La Flamingo.

La Flamingo.

It is the dance isn't it? La Flamingo.
That dalliance, between Del Negro Italiano
And the Spanish Abella, whereupon bare
they lay their souls.

La Flamingo.

La Flamingo.

No darker the light can Del Negro be
Beside the moonlit night of a Spanish sea.
As tender as a cantaloupe can be, Abella,
Del Negro Italiano she longs to please.

La Flamingo.

La Flamingo.

That dalliance, between Del Negro Italiano
And the Spanish Abella, whereupon bare
they lay their souls.

La Flamingo.

La Flamingo.

Paragon Of Modest Virtue

How often are you alone
in the world—your world? To be so
is well-chosen. Look twice
and you'll see your worlds differently.
It's something you'll never forget.

The wedding of the two, with their
distinct characteristics and beliefs
are discernible, when accentual,
and a paragon of modest virtue.

Sometimes

Sometimes

my eyes ache for that which they cannot
see,
my hands grasp for what they cannot
touch,
my heart for what it cannot
feel:

What they want

is you.

Daisy Pink Dresses

Masquerading in daisy pink dresses,
ruffled hems, and spaghetti straps,
are befuddled white girls
of Irish descent. Who, although bedazzling,
bleed green inside. While violins play,
they dream of bagpipes and Irish boys named Shaun,
folktales told by Irishmen swilling whiskey and beer,
the box guitar strumming the liar's lie.

Barefoot and pregnant they long to be. They do!
Adding to the O'Malley clan is an honor,
not a disgrace they know. Marry me Shaun O'Malley,
marry me, one shouts!

But Shaun dreams of Irish land, where
the air smells of sea vast and pure; of fields
wet with dirt ripe for planting. It's the soiled hands
of a man that makes him a man he sighs.
For Shaun wants his own land, with an Irish woman,
who never masquerades in a daisy pink dress,
ruffled hem, spaghetti strap, and a befuddled look.
Not even a chorus girl. But an Irish girl,
who bleeds green.

Sugar Cookie

The sugar cookie crumbles
in the entrance of my mouth

as my teeth, like Saber-tooth
tiger teeth, make short work

of a much needed ingest.

Its sweetness, the cookie's
sweetness, lingers on my

palette and in-between my
lips, pleasing me like a

tongue probing French Kiss
that teases the deep, dark,

recess of my mouth.

A French Kiss? It's the only
thing sweeter than a sugar
cookie.

The Finger Of God

I am never privy to the sounds of my own sleep,
and neither is my lover, who talks in hers, mentioning
his names in blissful moans, as if sniffing the
aromatic aroma of a hot double caramel latte from a
paper cup with a four-leaf clover etched on its spine.

The crease of her spine I trace, not with imagination,
but my middle finger, the one I use to cause her
fountain to erupt like contrails extending across the
light blue sky, as her eyes roll upward like bars on
slot machines; as her mouth opens wide like a
canyon, exhaling breath in a manner suggesting she's
touched the face of God.

Only, she knows, I am the finger of God.

GOD

Settling upon the horizon
is an endearing expression,
neither misplaced nor lost;

but enduring, perpetually
galvanizing; arising out of
presence of forethought,

fashioned with intent;
seized upon, not by the
good graces of wishful

thinking; but the watchful
eyes of an ever-unfolding
manifestation of God.

140 Characters

Him—*the Creator*, spoke,

When silent the cosmos stood.

Tweeted suddenly were

140 characters; unleashing,

The beginning of the end.

Heaven Is A Lofty Place

Never underestimate competition. Always remember the quick and nimble competitor. Primarily, the very

religious, who keep score by pointing to the sky. For Heaven is a lofty place, where such tribute is paid to a

tributary; the giver of power and strength. Pointing is neither an affirmation of toughness or pride; but faith.

Once understood – winning means everything.

Lady Lewis

Lovely is the light and life of Lady Lewis.
Like a lark lingering before the rise of night,

before the bishop of her soul, the earthly bishop
who makes her whole, the whole congregation

that loves her saintly soul. Lovely is

Lady Lewis.

Fairest among all the flowers of the field,
finer than the finest of silk revealed, more glorious

than the taste of aged wine. Such is Lady Lewis.
For Bishop knows. Bishop Lewis knows,

lovely is the light and life of

Lady Lewis.

Tethys

Driftwood never makes for a good relationship, given
the demagoguery of sea current. Trade winds are
seldom negotiable, for they are far too unpredictable
of tumult.

Help lovers lost at sea, Tethys.

If beached whales, like sea faring mariners,
on occasion lose their way; what then is to be said
of star-crossed lovers?

It's a terrible thing to be lost at sea, Tethys.

Driftwood never puts up a fuss. It knows the surge
will eventually roll in. When as the morrow, bleached
in the furrow of the hot sun, a night's fire comes;
whereby, warmth is homely, and the rushing
waves—spellbinding.

Has driftwood ever been truly lost at sea, Tethys?

Unconsolable

from the sky
fell
the unconsolable tear

full of salt
filled with sea
freely

no contrail
bearing no tale
to tell

Just

unconsolable

the tear

fell

An Open Field

We do not spring forth from the earth
Although, in time, it summons us

Where we take to rest
In an open field

Where freshly cut flowers are there to lie
Beside us and our newfound neighbors

The ones sleeping
All around us

In the midst of our neatly manicured lawn
Permanent is this our new neighborhood

Where sleep is peaceful
And rest—eternal

Figments & Figurines

my mother is old
as is my father

they are dying
as we all are

I waive at them
as they pass bye

for they understand
I am them—

and they are me

soon, they'll become
figments and figurines

family filament
illuminating my life

encased in menageries
of modest memory

so I waive at them
as they pass bye

for they understand
I am them—

and they are me
figments and figurines

All Men Toil

Some men toil in open vanity

Some men toil in blind conceit

Some toil in mincing memories

Nevertheless, all men toil

Junkie

The other day,
I saw a man sifting through a trash can.
he wasn't hungry,
he was just looking.

I'm told by some,
one man's junk is another man's treasure;
therefore, this junkie must be a rich man.

How vain we are—
when we look down on such people.
the trash in the can was deep,
my perception of value—shallow.

Today,
I saw a man sifting through a trash can.
he wasn't hungry—
he was just looking.

Conflation

i egged him
that unsuspecting man
walking down 82nd avenue
on his way somewhere
to see someone
i still see the egg exploding on his chest
i still hear the egg bursting on his chest
i still see his arms
spreading like feathers
on a puffed up peacock

a habitual liar is my mother
so I grew up loathing lying
a black widow spider she is not
that would not do her justice
she is a scorpion; and I,
because of her lies
have become a Saint

i egged him.
that unsuspecting man
to this day, he doesn't know
who I am

Night Train

Night train
Rumbles past my window
Luminous in a sudden

Shadow

Earthshaking the rattling
Like rock music the rolling
Clacking in rhythmic

Fashion

Absent the certainty of caption
This prince of darkness
That phantom

Of the third watch

Night train

57′ Chevy

She
always
seduces me;

that
backseat
of her

57' Chevy

Naïve

A twisted phrase

A missing left wing

Margins on a page

When dogs sing

Barack Obama

A drug-induced haze

Sex toys

A hand half raised

Altar boys

Anna Nicole Smith

Freedom of speech

The rhythm method

A lying leech

A cold rod

George W. Bush

Light Beer

A Two-State solution

The Race for the Cure

American Exceptionalism

John Lennon

A first kiss

Trickle-Down Economics

3 wishes

Ebonics

Halle Berry

A poetry teacher

Romeo and Juliet

Young preachers

A casino bet

Naïve

In An Age of Rage

In an age of rage we never find rage roadside, housed in an icebox
outside a filling station, remotely located in the desert a hundred miles away

from the multi-spring water fountain in the heart of town, where two women
lock horns over the same female lover; while a group of men place bets

in the background.

"Baby killers" yell First Baptist congregants at the Planned Parenthood Clinic
on 5th and Main. "Turn or Burn" on protest signs are emblematic in an age

of rage, where kill before letting be killed is viewed as a justifiable homicide
in the righteous name of the God of the Bible. Onward Christian soldier

they sing in an age of rage.

Unbeknown to the townspeople a race riot will rage throughout the night
wherein stores will be looted, businesses burned, and people die because a

young white woman falsely accuses a Black man of kidnapping her baby,

just because her boyfriend said he was leaving her for
a Black woman.

Neo-Nazi sympathizers gather to swill beer and yell
racial epithets at the
television, all the while afraid to go out into the
streets for fear, even though

they have shaven heads, and swastikas tattooed on
their arms and chests,
and steel-toed black boots laced shin high. Nothing is
like the ignorant thought

of a steel-toed boot on the back of a person's neck to
appease the bigotry
of a White racist pig.

Run little Shepherd boy run. Run because you like
boys in an age of rage.
Where is the righteous rage in this age of rage? Whose
rage will rise

and protect him

from violence? Who will defend his innocence? When
will the rage of the
law leap from the pages into the streets with justice in
tow? Rest in peace now

you, the Shepherd's boy, in an age of rage—in an age
of rage.

In My City

There are Black
people in my city. They are
everywhere now. But there's
no Black community, no NAACP,
no Urban League,
that's making
a real difference,
in
my city.

There are
Black churches. Not many
White people attend them.
They go
elsewhere. To
Multnomah Falls, and
Timothy Lake, Mt. Hood and
Lincoln City, and seaside;
to yard-work and garage sales,
Trailblazer games, their kids
soccer matches and festivals,
and any place
other than
the Black church,
in
my city.

The jazz world, and the
R&B world,
in my city is
amazing! Linda Hornbuckle,

she's big league, big voiced,
and a beautiful
Black women.
Soulful saxophonist
Patrick Lamb,
that White boy! He's got to be
Black; I just know it!
And Mel Brown, the
legend, the master,
he's vintage!

Then there's
my musician friends: Gordon Lee,
jazz pianist extraordinaire;
legendary bassist, Andre St. James;
my man, drummer, Edwin Coleman;
jazz pianist Ramsey Embick; and
the hardest, smartest, and multitalented
saxophonist, producer, and
record label owner,
Mr. Noah Peterson,
in
my city.

The Trailblazers are
my city's team. Nate McMillan is
a great coach. Paul Allen, the owner
should retain him. If
they win the championship, it
will have been
a good decision.
Some love the Timbers. Love
for them is growing.

It won't be long before, they'll
become—beloved,
in
my city.

I love my city.

Last Thursday

Last Thursday, an Asian woman waited on me. She was beautiful. She was of medium height and a thin build. Her face masked a facade of anger so pretentious I found it both sensuous and self-serving. I understood it; I was acquainted with it, that façade, her contrived sense of anger.

She was protecting herself. She was exercising self-preservation, something honed from puberty, from years wherein people measured her, judged her, called into question her virtue.

Because she was waitstaff, she knew, at least for the moment, she was less than. But to me, I found her greater than. Greater than the leering eyes she feels when filling empty water glasses, when serving guests the main entree, when petitioned for tea and soda that's not optional. I understood that. Having been waitstaff, I was acquainted with that.

So, I did something uncommon, something extraordinary. I moved the chair next to me. This gave her access to my table where empty water glasses waited. No one else seated around the table gave her the time of day. No one was swayed to help her find a way to make her work easier.

And then it happened. She did something uncommon, something extraordinary. She turns to me and says in a firm and affirming voice "Thank you."

Last Thursday, an Asian woman waited on me. She was beautiful. She was of medium height and a thin build. Her face masked a facade of anger so pretentious I found it both sensuous and self-serving. I understood it; I was acquainted with it, that facade, her contrived sense of anger.

She was protecting herself. She was exercising self-preservation, something honed from puberty, from years wherein men and women measured her, judged her, called into question her virtue.

But on last Thursday, for one moment, for me, and for me alone, she removed her mask, her facade, her contrived sense of anger, when she said, "Thank you."

Twin Fools

Twin fools does the argument make
Less the reasoned soul who walks away
Taking with him sanity for name sake
Until dusk filled dawn ends the fray

Unkind Woman

Unkind woman.

Thou art every-bit
the witch.
That includes the
marked distinction
of self serving bitch.

Ye unkind woman
saith the parish priest.

Life Begins In The Womb

When shall the poet sell the soul?
When tempted?
Embellished by lust?
Or, impoverished by the fleeting fortunes
Of fame?

Life begins in the womb. Soon,
Innate desires make themselves known.
But what of the soul? The heart
In matters thereof?

An infant's cry is the selling of hunger,
The need to be changed, to be held.
Then comes knowledge and reason,
Followed by passion and rationale.
There exists the need to know
And to be known.

Life is nothing more than poetics.
Singular stories of the soul woven into
Complex narratives stolen by poets,
The secular prophets in human existence.
When then shall the poet sell the soul, or
Was it ever for sale?

Temptations rise and fall,
Embellished lusts burst like bubbles, and
Fame comes as quickly as fortunes go.

Life begins in the womb; not in the
Poet's pen.

Moon Sang

In middle the Yangtze stands an almond tree. Of the two which one will bow? Who will empty his cup? The tree, or the Yangtze asks the Sifu?

A puzzled look adorns the new Moon Sang.

The answer to the riddle is this says the Sifu. The Yangtze will steer clear of provocation. Bow and do likewise.

Life Is Larger Here

Open spaces overwhelm me
Where purple pigeons pace
Bobbing in fruitful futility
Giving rhythm its reason
And me, a subtle sense of
Awe

Life is larger here
Where fluffy is cotton candy
Picked with sticky fingers
Licked with icky tongues
And me, lost in the frothy
Moment

Water fountains flow freely
Like gods from ancient antiquity
Beseeching me to boldly bow
In this a timeless open space
Where I, bless these gods with
Thirst

Open spaces overwhelm me
Where costumed clowns clown
Floating fully filled balloons
Held by happy little children
While I, watch with such
Wonder

Life is larger here
Where warm lattes wait
For patrons to purchase

Where weary worn men
Like me, wait for each new
Moment

Why here oh you heavens
Where I opine in open space
Where I am overwhelmed
By this sense of certain grief
In me, as I contemplate my
Shadow

Life is larger here

City Boy

A boy

leaves for school.

He

does not return.

They found

his bicycle.

They found

his book-bag.

They found his coat.

They found

him,

playing baseball,

at the park.

I love

my city.

Every Time I Go Away

Every time
I go away
something comes
a letter, a visitor, a friend

Every time
I go away
something goes
the toilet, the faucet, the dog

Every time
I go away
some things wait
my life, my wife, my children

Every time
I go away
some things remain
faith, hope, and love

Every time
I go away

And I Smiled

This morning's sun
smiled upon my face,
wherein I awoke,
just in time to note,
the width of it,
the pith of it,
deep the depth of it.

And I smiled.

Defiance

children, are dying, daily
without deliberation, death comes
to Somali children
to Sudanese children
the Horn of Africa's children
they are dying
where they are hungry
they are starving
malnourished and thirsty
children lay dying
scorched by heat
pestered by flies
in arms of mothers
before the eyes of fathers
next to extended stomachs
of brother and sister
while people in America
stand ready in defiance
over Roe vs. Wade
as children die, daily

Animus

Embers of animus still swirl wildly
In the pit of my heart I find no coals to burn
If there had been an ash-pit I'd known of it
Every fire laden with angst requires a flame
Towering tall and long is its flicker
Crackle, snap, pop gives rise to voice
From the amber colored flame they speak
Fire is known for its burn not its sting
What animal is filled with such animus
When you meet one ask it that question
Do I dare say you'll get an answer
They don't think in such vitriolic terms
We humans are the strange ones
We are so animated in our animus
Ill-will is contrary to our well-being
Anally retentive is our impassioned animus
In what pit did we extinguish esteem
For animus sake we've purged goodwill
Swirl wildly embers swirl wildly

Bataan

The pride of man neither changes nor exfoliates: If deviant was not a derivative of divergent, he'd still know it.

Man is the crowned jewel on creations diadem: Oh the destruction he advances with his clenched fists.

Man to his end marches as if summoned by Bataan cadence: As if taken by force he yields to the inevitable.

Man's end-state is not pessimism, but a foregone conclusion: Who can save him from the deception of his own self?

Man?

Steinway On The Steel Bridge

On the Steel Bridge is Steinway.
He sits there alone on the walkway, facing
south, where the Hawthorne Bridge stands tall
and wide, luminous like a fading structure
no longer viewed as modern architecture.

Steinway is deeply black—polished black,
with piano keys white like akoya pearls.

There, in silence, he waits for me on the
Steel Bridge, above the Columbia River, as the
slow currents give tow; where cars and trains
pass bye, and the people look, and children
wave goodbye, as they travel to somewhere,
amused by me and Steinway, on the

Steel Bridge.

Solace

I find solace in quiet

A respite from the storms

Of voice—

Such reverence

Life Is Good

Rain fell today
No one got wet
We were all inside
Sipping tea
Eating crumpets

Now I'm home
Why
Rain fell today
I didn't get wet
Life is good

Milepost 7

Milepost 7,
is exactly 7 miles
from a fixed point
of reference.

Nearby,
7 families occupy
7 farm houses;
where 7 boys milk
7 cows, 7 days a
week, at 7
in the morning.

Daily,
7 girls, pick 7
daisies, hoping
the 7 boys
will notice them
when at
the bus stop
near
Milepost 7

Luck

When might a man find luck?

Is it when he's come upon a penny,
received a negative cancer diagnosis,

violates the rules governing traffic lights,
his wife says yes to his sexual advance,

exceeds legal limits for alcohol consumption,
then successfully navigates his way home
while under the influence?

What can be said of luck then?

Can any man say for certain?

Yes.

Bloomers

wearing a skirt
was a man
i think

quite the luminary
he was
i think

he took no thought
of his skirt
it seemed

was he wearing bloomers
most-likely
i think

but then again
maybe not

On A Sad Day

On a sad day we tell our stories
of risk and surprise, of life and loss,
of having won, even in the midst of defeat.

We war with each other, with ourselves,
with the internal conflicts found in conscience,
with the enmity in relationships.

Still, we find time to sing, sing the old song,
the new song, to pray, to recite endearing terms
of love, of longing, those songs of passion,
on a sad day.

Indifference

A Tri-Met bus just passed by
Saturday's route predetermined
I see dismembered leaves
Swirling in whirlwinds on MLK Jr. Blvd

Occasionally its trees shimmer shake
As if to signal the passing of summer
Not one passing car honk's an affirmation
So, to stillness do these trees return

Me? I sit in this here coffee shop
How ironic. It's name—Elevated Coffee
Elevated is the name of MLK Jr.
Not one passing car honk's in affirmation

Classical SiriusXM Radio plays quietly
Subconsciously I find myself listening
I'm certain the singer wants me to
But right now I'm into this poem

Both boulevard sidewalks are empty
Refusing to make space for shadows of *Fall*
Another Tri-Met bus just passed by
So what it's the same bus

You Still A Pig

I call you a racist
You call me a pig
Let's split the difference
I don't wear lipstick
And neither do pigs
Why hog everything?
Leave some space
For love
Pull from the top
Not the bottom
The paper—
Two-ply
The gum
Already been chewed
What gum
The one keeping us
Together
You still a pig
And you a racist
Wink
Oink!

An Unmasked Smile

She wore that smudge like a smile; something only
makeup unmasks. His finger poke to her face

points that out, the smudge that is.

And her smile, all the while something disingenuous.

His finger carried caustically his castigation. Her
smile,
the sole instrument of her insurrection, as his vitriol

maintained its virulence.

How long has he been the shepherd of such shearing,
and she that lamb led to slaughter, whose whimpered

whispers of rebuttal have long since gone silent.

The salient nature of her smile is spellbinding. Pithy
is the steely disposition of her silent strength, forged

in the pit of repeated heated castigation. But now,

she is free. And the smudge, an unmasked smile.

Clenched Fist

We clench our fist,

as if brave.

We are not.

We are fools;

who will be dead;

we the brave,

with our clenched fist.

Charlotte

From somewhere on the freeway a rock leaped up, like a Jack-in-the-Box, like a burlesques dancer on his birthday.

Rocks like that frighten him; burlesques dancers don't.

Much to his surprise the windshield didn't crack. Although, he did break-wind somewhere along the fault-line that constitutes the crack of his fat ass.

No spider like web appeared on the windshield. He asked Charlotte, the burlesques dancer seated next to him "Did you see that!" "No" she replied. "I'm on the World Wide Web right now."

He thought to himself, "Geeez!"

Environmentally Friendly

I asked her to wear a Naeem Khan gown. "Make it happen,"
I said. "No one wears one better." She felt special.

These days the single life gets crowded—especially in Cleveland.

The thought of such an appearance is the exclusive domain of fine women. What a special gift, and the best place to observe it, as are the legs and breasts of a shapely woman in a Naeem Khan gown.

There is something to being a sex symbol. Although, some say it sucks. Her real name is Chase. Chase me being the essence of her moniker—given the fact she's so difficult to manage.

Long live—imagination.

Whenever she is around there's loose talk. If not for love— I'd find her to be a lonely person.

She's what I liked when I was 16. Light eyes, short with cropped hair. A veiled smile, in the haze of the blue hour, was visible only to me.

For certain, that's what I thought to be true.

Yet, proof is relegated to performance. And oh how she could perform in that Naeem Khan gown.

In those moments she always challenged what's possible. Instantly, fashion savvy men wanted to know more about her. Lust stimulated their lascivious mind and unpretentious bravado.

All she would say is "I'm dressed for work." And, to a man— they would chuckle. Metaphorically speaking, I wondered, if they thought to themselves,

"Every dinner needs a great centerpiece."

What a hair-raising moment that would be for her. Honestly, I would never characterize such a metaphoric moment as,

"environmentally friendly,"

for any woman in a Naeem Khan gown. It's a fact, she is what makes a Naeem Khan gown—

beautiful.

A Beautiful Tragedy

This is a beautiful tragedy.
His Twitter bio lists his current job title,
an agreement reached with the opposition—
without national consensus.

At the press conference
it was brought up. One message rang loud
and clear, it's time to pause and shut out
everyday mutterings. Vote for life. Although,
it's more complicated than that.

We've deleted our judgment, which
reinforces the point—it's time to pause.
He suggests a restructuring plan, because
foreseeable is the loss of a decade.

"We need to take the power back, he exclaims!
If we don't the bonuses will be smaller
from year to year." But others say,
"Just let them expire—the years that is."

This is a beautiful tragedy.

Midnight In Madrid

What connects us to the authentic presence of a
nation?
Is it its people, an understanding of their history, their
culture,
or maybe one's own self?

What must take place to make good on an old
promise? Is it
to rest where the green grass is greener, or fences
made of
literal and figurative metaphors?

How nice it would be to sip tea outside a teashop in
Sydney,
and tell stories of what it's like to be an immigrant of
African
descent. Advance preparation is not necessary.

In everything there is a coherent thought if you
would just
listen for it. Its legroom isn't just for exit rows
anymore. Why?
Compassion has and always will be comforting.

I love seeing art in streets. San Francisco,
Philadelphia,
and Brussels are great places to view such expressions
of
creativity. Where have you been lately?

It takes time to fall in love with a destination. Tap the world
of its vast knowledge and study the cultures therein. For you'll
enjoy how much everywhere else gives you.

Stroll through the multicultural heritage, discover and enjoy
the uniqueness of the hidden world. Experience the presence
of the people the pen and paper describe.

Leave the ordinary behind. It's time to be in harmony with
nature, and in tune with culture, especially not your own. It
will direct you to interesting conversations.

At midnight in Madrid, everyone eats twelve grapes, one by
one, in keeping with their clock's chime. Having done so,
in sync with the clock, foreshadows prosperity and good luck.

Never turn back the hands on a clock when it keeps time.
For life stops for no one. Only upon their death. Therein a
journey begins of unimaginable proportion.

Something Curious

I'm sure most of you are well aware
many consider stars a wonder of the cosmos,
so get to know the night sky and perfect its image.

I was happily surprised just counting naked-eyed
stars,
while a mandolin played ever so lightly through the
night.
It turned out nicely considering my amateur musing.

Has anyone wondered how many civilizations lurk
in the cosmos? Will they someday lead to our demise?
How picture perfect that would be.

Some books ignore the galaxies. The logic — behind
such
omission — might alter a close encounter someday.
Yet —
that encounter, if it were to happen, would be

the toast of the town someday.

With the sun growing ten percent hotter, the earth,
over time — will become uninhabitable for us humans.

For some unexplainable reason maybe the alligators,
rattlesnakes, and red-tailed hawks, living north of the
Florida Everglades, on Seminole land, might survive:

The Seminoles were superstitious that way.

In the beginning of time the originalists were
minimalists. More landscape was preserved that way.
Now that's positive energy.

Traveling off the coast of Baja California
a gray baleen whale might surface for a brief whistle,
but who among men will hear it, let alone see it?

For he and the human family will have long gone
underground.

What would a woman in love—living under the earth
give
to see a lone mute swan stretch its wings in the dawn
of the
rising morning?

There's one for everyone—that image—those fleeting
images

of the once archetypal ecosystem. Clearly the long winter
of man's terrestrial living will have since passed.

Point your eyes at something and then try to make sense of it.
Something curious might happen. The experience — a thing pertaining to life.

And the wonder — who knows?

Small World

We have proved the power of small, having conquered our expectations by reducing everything in our awe into manageable proportions. And our world became the better for it.

Beyond Me

If I could peer into the future
I would
Not knowing what I'll see
Looking beyond me
To others
To fellow man
To the condition of woman
To the aspiration of children

Will the planet be alive
Its ecosystem have survived
Will the world as we know it
thrive

Even among the races
Will I find
There still exists
The big divide

Will I be able to chide
My hope for one civilization
Where the color of face doesn't matter
Where religious preference
Is no longer a factor that matters

Where all religions
live in peace
Where political parties
Sit down and smoke their peace
Taking a lesson from the past
From the Native American people

Who long ago passed
Before
What I see

Beyond me

The Opal Looking Sky

Above the opal looking sky
In celestial worlds beyond my eyes
Is there life there
Is there another me somewhere
Who dreams of places he's never been
Of worlds to which I will never go
Do we wonder
Is there life there
Above the opal looking sky

Draw Something

"Draw something" I said.
And with one stroke she traced her heart
over the surface of my mine.

And I loved her for it.

"Draw something" she said. And I
stroked twelve concentric shaped hearts
before her eyes.

And she loved me for it.

On that day my heart skipped a beat;
and the twelve concentric hearts never melted
in the warmth of her eyes.

Draw something.

Graffiti

like graffiti,
scribbled writing means something
in the eyes, and from the hand
of a child.

its patterns,
every stroke, decoupled from
intent and cognitive imagination,
comes from somewhere
as desire dictated by
impulse.

without border,
the lines flow like wild rivers
unabridged by
banks with ambiguous lines
only paper reveals.

in time,
the scribbling will conform
to structure, by design,
tempered after countless hours
of repetitive practice.

in time, the world will
become bigger,
giving rise to form, syntax,
and glyphic.
scribble my child, scribble
big; for I,
am waiting.

In The Dark

After plucking out my eyes
I was still blind
Speckled light flickered
I was speechless
My form was present but inaudible
We were both dumbfounded
Tussling in the dark
Crisscrossing each other's boundaries
Until I awoke from sleep
Seething and sweaty

Torment

Within wild leaves wrestles torment
Coming together a matter of consequence
And lament
Forlorn forces of nature forge moments
As incessant winds whine loudly
Without relent
Cascading downhill like cartwheels
Bitterly exchanging positions
Engaged in acrobatic drills
Vagrants are democratic ideals
Given the totalitarian nature of wind
Loose leaves know to kneel
We wrestle like leaves in wind
Whining during rise of the same
Where does it begin and end

Waltz

Waltzing its way downhill is rainwater
Soothing the fluidity of my senses
Washing away my worrisome wonders
Until that beached whale appeared

Shame On The Cocoa Bean

Oddly enough, there are clouds in my coffee
Floating like lily pads toads tend to leap from
Just before whirlwinds gather the makings of a storm
Shame on the cocoa bean for surrendering its essence
Allowing itself to be liquidated like Icelandic ice
But with a Nubian color and chocolate disposition
Somehow these clouds buck the Starbucks blend
Causing me to wonder if these clouds ever existed
In a 16 oz cup of Café Americano brand coffee
The Italian barista understands this kind of saying
For he has his brew brewing with steam the likes of
Geysers arising from the ash-laden lips of Pinatubo
Oddly enough, it's cloudy there

Tumult

Somewhere
Beneath this brown veneer

Where
Sanguine blood stirs

Certainly
Spirit & just soul concur

Erring
In idyllic conflict

Dictated
By inharmonic dichotomy

Between
White the interior
And
Brown the veneer

Is
Great tumult

Bards

As wild as our wildest imaginations may be,
we are serfs of sense and sensibility. Civil in
servitude,

saintly in devotion, of Celtic order; we recite dutifully
the dalliances of poetic dictation dancing wildly in
whimsical verse. With harp in hand, we recite
lyrically,

the epic, the heroic, the tragic poem. For we are bards,
male and female, we are bards.

Close The Door Gently

This, an open door
leads to an unwritten poem,
somewhere in the well
of your imagination.

Close the door gently.
Write the poem,
slowly; savoring
every word,
and every image.

Go there.

Beyond the page,
into the distant world,
the intangible realm,
that metaphysical place.

It's safe there.

How do I know this?
Close the door gently.

Ostensibly

I write what few people read.
I speak what many seldom hear.
I record what only I play.
I see what others refuse to believe.
If I quit, everyone will wonder
Where I went. Ostensibly –
I will have went nowhere.

Remains the Day

Is there any poetry to be written today?

To self:

I don't know, there still remains the day.

ABOUT THE AUTHOR

emmett wheatfall lives in Portland, Oregon where he reads, writes, and performs poetry. He has published two books of poetry entitled *He Sees Things* (2010) and *We Think We Know* (2011).

He has published four chapbooks under the titles *Queen of the Nile, I Too Am A Slave, The Majestic,* and *Midnight In Madrid* through Portland publishing company Naviguer Les Mers Publishing. A number of his poems have been published by online journals and periodicals.

He has released two lyrical poetry CDs. *When I Was Young* (2010) is a highly regarded thematic CD that speaks to love, hope, betrayal, and fidelity addressed in various social and cultural context. *I Loved You Once* (2011) contains great poetry writing set to jazz, blues, and pop musical influences.

emmett has performed lyrical poetry at Jimmy Maks, a premier Northwest Jazz club and one of America's top 100 Jazz clubs. Accompanied by world class Jazz musicians in the persons of Noah Peterson, Gordon Lee, Andre St. James, Edwin Coleman, and Ramsey Embick, he has performed lyrical poetry for sold out audiences.

In addition, he has read and performed lyrical poetry in concert with Oregon Poet Laureate Lawson Inada, and is an active participant in the Portland Poetry Slam (PPS) spoken word scene.

emmett is a signed recording artist with Peterson Entertainment, Inc.

P.O. Box 30105
Portland, Oregon 97294
Phone: (503) 501-6140

BOOK ORDER FORM

Please fill in your full name, company name (if applicable), shipping address, phone number, and e-mail address below.

NAME:	SHIPPING ADDRESS:
PHONE:	
EMAIL:	

DESCRIPTION	PRICE	QUANTITY	TOTAL
Book – The Meaning of Me	$15.00		
Book – He Sees Things	$15.00		
Book – We Think We Know	$15.00		
Chapbook – Midnight in Madrid	$5.00		
Chapbook – Queen of the Nile	$5.00		
Chapbook – I Too am a Slave	$5.00		
Chapbook – The Majestic	$5.00		
	SUBTOTAL		
	SALES TAX		
	SHIPPING & HANDLING (QUANTITY x $2.00)		
	EXPEDITED PRIORITY + $10.00 OVERNIGHT + $20.00		
	TOTAL		

Orders will ship within 1-2 business days after receipt of cleared payment.

Make checks payable to: emmett wheatfall

Electronic payments can be made online through http://emmettwheatfall.com or http:///paypal.com
PayPal id: ewcle@yahoo.com

CPSIA information can be obtained at www.ICGtesting.com
Printed in the USA
BVOW011602120712

294964BV00007B/2/P

9 780983 723141